Coffee And Kisses

A collection of poems on love and loss,
motherhood and messy friendship,
unspoken words, midnight thoughts, and
coffee dates that healed more than therapy.

Mamta Vaswani Sood

Made with ❤ on the BookLeaf Publishing Platform
www.bookleafpub.in
www.bookleafpub.com

Dedication

To Shanaya — my giggling, wriggling, bundle of joy, drool, and surprise diaper explosions.
To Aayush — for your endless patience, love, and ability to find my phone when it's literally in my hand.
Wouldn't do this life and this book without you two.
And to coffee — without you, this book (and most of my sentences) wouldn't exist.

We did this, team.

Preface

This book is written with the hope of offering a voice to those whose words have remained trapped within them, unspoken but deeply felt. It is for the ones who have carried their stories in silence, unsure of how to shape them into sentences, or perhaps afraid that no one would truly understand. Between these pages, you will find pieces of poetry that are more than just ink on paper ,they are fragments of untold emotions, altered and molded so that each person who reads them might find a piece of themselves reflected back.

Every poem in this collection has been shaped with care and intention, designed to touch the many faces of love and connection that exist in our lives. It is written for the lover who pours their heart out in glances and small gestures, whose affection runs deep even when words fail. It is for the friend who remains steady and true, offering comfort not always in grand declarations but in quiet presence and unwavering loyalty. It is for the mother who gives endlessly, whose sacrifices are often hidden behind smiles and whose love is a constant current, even when it goes unnoticed by the world. And it is for the introvert, the soul who may struggle to say what they feel aloud, but whose eyes tell stories of love, longing, and unspoken dreams more powerfully than words ever could.

This collection is an offering to every person who has ever loved in silence, to every heart that has felt deeply but spoken softly. It is a place where your hidden feelings might finally find form, where your quiet stories are not only heard but honored. Here, every verse is a mirror to the emotions that live within you, waiting to be seen and acknowledged. So may you find solace in these poems, may they remind you that even the softest voices and the quietest hearts have a place in the world, and that their love, though unspoken, is no less powerful or true.

Acknowledgements

This book holds a special corner in my heart. It is not just a collection of poems, but a gathering of moments that have been inspired, deeply felt, and quietly observed over time. Every word, every line has its roots in real emotions and lived experiences. And as I bring this work into the world, I am filled with gratitude for the people and connections that have made this journey possible.

First and foremost, I want to thank my daughter for giving me the profound honour of being her mother. Through her, I have come to truly feel the depth and beauty of motherhood. She has been my greatest teacher, showing me new dimensions of love, patience, and wonder that I might never have discovered on my own. Every smile, every challenge, every little milestone has enriched my soul and found its way, quietly but powerfully, into the words I write.

To my husband, I owe endless gratitude. He has stood beside me like a rock, steady, unwavering, and strong through every season of life. His silent strength and constant support have been my anchor, allowing me the freedom to create, to dream, and to pour my heart into these pages without fear. His belief in me, even in the quietest moments, has been a light that keeps me going.

I also want to thank my cherished coffee partner, whose companionship has added warmth and comfort to my days. Our shared conversations, laughter, and silences over countless cups have nourished my spirit more than words can say. These simple yet meaningful moments have become little sanctuaries where thoughts and feelings bloom many of which have found their way into this book.

And finally, to the people who have spoken volumes without uttering a word those whose eyes have said everything that lips could not. I see you, I hear you, and I thank you. It is in these silent exchanges, in the unsaid but deeply understood emotions, that I have found some of the richest inspiration. This book is, in many ways, a tribute to those unspoken connections that bind us in ways language often cannot capture.

With all my heart, I offer this collection as a reflection of all that I have seen, felt, and lived. May it touch those quiet corners of your own heart, just as these people and moments have.

1. My Baby Girl

To My Darling Shanaya

From the moment you came into my life,
A radiant star, my heart's delight.
My little daughter, my entire world,
In you, my love and dreams unfurled.

Each day unfolds a brand-new scene,
As you grow into all you're meant to be.
Your laughter, a melody so sweet,
Your steps, a rhythm, light and fleet.

I cherish every smile and glance,
The way you sing, the way you dance.
Your curious eyes that brightly gleam,
Reflecting hopes, and every dream.

Through scraped knees and tender tears,
Through triumphs, joys, and fleeting fears,
I'm honored to guide you on your way,
To watch you blossom day by day.

My precious Shanaya, always know,
No matter how much more you grow,

My love for you will never fade,
Forevermore, through time and space.

In storms that come, I'll be your shield,
With open arms, your heart to wield.
Together we'll dream, together we'll fly,
With each new challenge, just you and I.

So embrace the world with your shining light,
With every endeavor, reach wondrous height.
For in your spirit, I see the spark,
A boundless journey, where love leaves its mark.

2. When love wore pink

I saw him first beneath office lights,
a smile that warmed the coldest days,
eyes that spoke in quiet poems,
shoulders broad with gentle grace.

I wished for friendship, soft and shy
but fate had deeper dreams than I.
Love bloomed slow, like velvet rain,
a breeze that brushed away all pain.

He was Punjabi—bold, alive,
I, a Sindhi—rooted, bright.
Two souls, two songs, one perfect rhyme,
our cultures danced, our hearts kept time.

He asked, I smiled, my "yes" a flame,
beneath the sky that knew my name.
In pink I stood, December air,
and found forever in his stare.

No fire burned, no grand display
just prayers and peace to light the way.
And in his hands, a gift so small
a black cat, softest love of all.

Now every vow, each laugh we keep,
began that day—so wide, so deep.
The day my heart began to sing...
The day love wore soft shades of pink.

As seasons turned, our roots entwined,
each whispered dream, a thread defined.
Through storms we danced, through sunlit skies,
with trust that grew, a sweet surprise.

In quiet moments, hands intertwined,
a symphony that life aligned.
For every glance, each stolen breath,
a testament to love's own depth.

And as we walk this winding road,
with every step, our story flowed.
Together painted in hues so bold,
a tapestry of dreams retold.

3. The scent of us

Our love once lingered in the scent of coffee,
In morning light and midnight talks so softly.
Now those moments live in memory's glow,
A chapter closed, yet never let go.

They say time heals, and hearts will mend,
But I still carry you—my love, my friend.
Not as a wound, but a song in my chest,
You were the calm, the comfort, the rest.

I don't need to forget to feel free
For loving you was the cure in me.
And though you're gone, your love still stays,
Warming my soul in the quietest ways.

Like whispers of dreams that linger and weave,
In the fabric of life, you still make me believe.
Each sunset reminds me of laughter we shared,
In the silence, your echo is gently prepared.

With every dawn that breaks through the mist,
I'll hold you close in the moments I miss.
For love isn't lost, it simply transforms,
A timeless embrace that forever warms.

4. When I close my eyes

When I close my eyes to the hush of night,
After a life lived in love, in laughter, in light
The memories may fade, the details may stray,
Our coffee dates lost in the folds of the day.

I may forget my name, or the years we knew,
But one thing I'll seek as I slip into blue
Your fragrance, your presence, soft as a sigh,
To breathe you in once more, before your goodbye.

So when that moment gently arrives,
And the world grows quiet behind my eyes,
I hope you'll be there, just as you've always been
My beginning, my end, my forever within.

5. My favourite notification

It's 1 a.m., and silence fills the room,
Yet my heart stays awake, in quiet bloom.
I wait for that one gentle sign
A glow on my screen, his name in a line.

A face I can't see, but feel so near,
Hands I can't touch, yet hold me here.
Fingers trace pixels, not skin so warm,
Yet somehow his words still calm the storm.

They reach through the dark, soft and deep,
Cradling my soul until I fall asleep.
And as I drift into dreams so dim...
I wait for the next night
To think of him.

6. The day you were born

If I could return to the day you arrived,
To the moment the world felt truly alive,
I'd hold you closer, love you more,
More than even the stars could ever store.

I'd tuck you gently against my chest,
Feel your heartbeat, watch you rest.
Your eyes.. so new, so full of light
Would meet mine and make the world right.

Those tiny hands, now strong and wide,
Once reached for me with arms open wide.
Those little crawls that danced on the floor
Now run toward dreams I once wished for.

But if I could go back, just for a while,
I'd cradle you close with the softest smile,
And let your gaze find mine so deep
Until you sigh, and fall asleep.

7. More than just friends

Do you remember how we used to love?
It was never meant to be just friendship's name
We danced between moments, not needing a frame,
Two hearts speaking where words never came.

Do you recall how we used to kiss?
Not through emojis or fleeting screens,
But in the warmth of cold coffee sips,
And in the silence that lived in between.

Now I fear to reach for familiar hands,
The ones that once held coffee and me.
They call us just friends, but we knew the truth,
And the rest became quiet history.

8. Whispers of destiny

You once said that destiny had played its part,
But I believed we were painting our own stars
Writing our story with every breath we took,
Not bound by fate, but by the way you looked.

I thought love was ours to shape and keep,
A promise whispered in dreams and sleep.
Yet here I stand, with pages torn apart,
Still holding your name at the edge of my heart.

Beneath the twilight where shadows softly creep,
I search for the echoes of laughter we'd reap.
In the silence of night, your memory's spark,
Illuminates paths that lead to the dark.

But I gather the fragments, each word and sigh,
Weaving them gently where our dreams still lie.
For though time may challenge the bond that we made,
Your essence remains in the love we conveyed.

9. Remind me of Us

Can you remind me..

Of the days when time stood still in your arms,
When laughter lived softly between our words,
And love was simple, unspoken, and warm.

Remind me of the nights lit by moonlight,
Where our shadows danced and hearts felt free,
When your voice was the calm in the quiet,
And your presence was all I'd ever need.

Remind me how your lips, tasting of cold coffee,
Found mine like they were always meant to be.
Remind me I was yours, and you were mine
And this distance now is just a passing dream.

Remind me of the whispers shared like secrets,
The warmth of your hand fit perfectly in mine,
When forever felt like a promise unbroken,
And love was the compass that guided our time.

Can you remind me
Of the way the stars would guide our night walks,
As we chased constellations, lost in their glow,

When each passing moment felt like our own song,
And the world outside faded, just letting usflow.

10. We'll find us again

Long nights have softened into fleeting words,
Where laughter once lingered, silence now stirs.
Hearts once spoken through glances and grace,
Now echo as emojis, lost in their place.

The coffee dates we dreamed of with care,
Now drift like whispers through thinning air.
Was this the fate we couldn't outrun?
A story half-written, undone by the sun?

But love like ours doesn't simply fade
It rests, it waits, in memories made.
So here's my vow, through loss and through pain
Our legacy lives, and we'll find us again

11. They call me a girl mom

Too big to be little,
Too little to be big,
And I watch you grow,
Always trying to find where you fit
In this world,
And forever in my heart.

A tiny version of me, full of light and sass,
Exploring life as the moments pass.
And still, I pause and softly ask:
Have I truly been given this beautiful task?

To be your girl mom, what a gift, what grace,
To see the world through your curious face.

Thank you, my first love, my sweetest part,
My little teacher, my forever heart.
This bond we share, pure and true,
A lifetime of love, just me and you.

Grateful each day in every way,
For I always dreamed to be called your
Girl Mom
This way.

12. Mothering you

The battles I've fought, you'll never know,
The weight I've carried, I won't let show.
Your path will be lighter, your skies more clear,
For I'll guard your heart, hold you near.

You won't feel the sorrow that once touched me,
I'll wrap you in love, and let you be free
To laugh, to dream, to dance in the sun,
To grow in a world where joy has just begun.

You've given me more than I ever knew,
A chance to heal, to begin anew.
In mothering you, I've found my way
You've mothered me, in your own sweet way.

13. The shape of letting go

Is it possible to feel complete,
When your world is stitched with incompleteness?
To wear a smile that doesn't quite reach,
While carrying echoes of something you miss?

Is it possible to let go of the hands
You once vowed to hold for all time?
To watch love drift like sand through fingers,
And still believe you're doing fine?

Is it possible to un-love again,
To unwrite the verses etched so deep?
To quiet the heart that once only sang
For the name it now whispers in sleep?

. . .

Yes?
Perhaps.
But even then
The love, the loss,
It shapes us
Again
And again.

14. A cup of longing

Is it alright if I offer you a cup of coffee,
Knowing my fingers may never entwine with yours,
As they cradle the warmth meant to touch my soul?

To sit across from you in quiet reverie,
Watching steam rise like whispered confessions,
Bridging the space between your heart and mine.

Love doesn't always seek possession;
Sometimes, it's found in silent offerings
A cup of coffee, tenderly given,
An unspoken promise of enduring affection.

So let me love you in this gentle way,
With gestures that speak what words cannot say.
One cup, one moment, eternally true
A simple act of adoring you.

15. Cherished love

It began with simple, chance hellos,
Typed words that sparked where no one knows.
What started as random, fleeting talks,
Now paves the path my heart now walks.

Your messages, once casual, light,
Became my comfort every night.
In every word, a warmth I find,
A gentle touch upon my mind.

From scattered chats to something more,
You've become the one I most adore.
No longer just a distant friend,
But the very world where my dreams blend.

16. Unspoken mutual love

In the quiet moments before sleep, I'd wonder if you
thought of me,
Sending messages for coffee, just to see your face.
Yet, you saw me only as a friend,
While my heart yearned for more.

Years later, I bared my soul,
Confessing the love I'd long concealed.
Your eyes softened as you revealed,
Your feelings had mirrored mine all along.

Two hearts, each silent in their longing,
Passing like ships in the night.
If only we'd spoken sooner,
Our love might have found its light.

17. In another life

Perhaps in another life, I'm easier to love,
A gentler soul, fitting like a glove.
Beyond mere friendship, our hearts entwined,
In that realm where love's unconfined.

There, we fulfill what here we miss,
Sharing dreams sealed with a kiss.
I yearn to dream of that place anew,
Manifesting a world with you.

In another life, do you promise to be mine?

18. Heaven's gift

Before your first breath graced this land,
Angels pondered, hand in hand.
"Is the world prepared," they mused,
"For this precious soul, so infused?"

They painted skies with hues of dawn,
Ensured the path you'd tread upon.
With gentle whispers, set the scene,
For you, our child, our cherished dream.

We know your worth, profound and true,
A blessing rare, in all you do.
Forever grateful, hearts in plea,
To be your loving family.

19. Can love happen twice?

I don't want the old love,
If it were true, it wouldn't fade.
Real love doesn't vanish in silence,
It doesn't walk away, afraid.

I've found a new spark,
One that laughs with my soul.
He brings me sweet things and sweeter days,
And somehow, he makes me whole.

He reads the words I never say,
He holds the storms I hide.
With every tear he draws from me,
I feel more alive inside.

They say love comes once,
But I know that's not quite right
Because I've fallen again, deeply,
And this time, it feels like light.

So let the old love stay behind,
Like pages turned, like faded skies
This love is real, it's joy, it's pain,
And proof that love can happen twice.

20. A symphony of love

In the gentle glow of morning light,
Your laughter starts our day just right.
With tiny hands, our daughter plays,
A melody that brightens all our ways.

You bring me chocolates, sweet and fair,
A tender token of the love we share.
Desserts that melt upon my tongue,
Echoing the songs our hearts have sung.

In turn, I cook with love anew,
Crafting meals, a heartfelt brew.
Each dish a verse, each flavor tells,
The story that our union spells.

Together, we compose a life,
Harmonious notes as man and wife.
With our daughter, life's sweetest tune,
Our family, under love's bright moon.

Through bites of chocolate, meals we make,
In every step, the paths we take,
Our love's a feast, both sweet and true,
A symphony composed by me and you.

21. Our harmonious blend

In our daughter's face, your features reside,
Lips curved like yours, a familial pride.
Yet in her eyes, my spirit gleams,
A fusion of our shared dreams.

Her hair cascades in waves like mine,
A flowing testament of our entwined line.
But in her stance, your essence shows,
A balanced blend that gently glows.

Family whispers, "She's both combined,
A perfect duo, intertwined."
A fairy dancing in delight,
Our hearts embrace this joyous sight.

In her, our worlds unite as one,
A living proof of love begun.
Our daughter, cherished, ever dear,
Embodiment of all we hold near.

22. Unnoticed affection

25

In the glow of café lights, I sat across from you,
My heart quietly reaching out.
You shared your thoughts, your dreams,
Unaware of the silent longing in my eyes.

I offered my friendship openly,
Hoping you'd see the depth beneath.
But my feelings remained unseen,
And my heart quietly retreated.

23. Escape with you

My dearest companion, my heart's delight,
Let's leave behind the city's light.
To paths unknown, where dreams reside,
With you, my love, right by my side.

In cozy nooks of distant lands,
We'll sip our coffee, hands in hands.
The world outside may fade away,
As we embrace the break of day.

Through whispered winds and skies of blue,
Every journey leads me to you.
Let's weave new memories, just us two,
My coffee partner, forever true.

24. Only once

I'm excited to watch you grow
to see your world expand,
your wonder bloom,
your light become.

But it hurts,
deep in places I never knew existed,
that I only get to do it once.

Just once
to hold you this small,
to hear your laughter echo like sunlight,
to lift you in my arms
as if I could keep time still.

Every day,
you become someone new.
Jumping higher,
laughing louder,
learning faster than I can catch.

And tomorrow,
you'll be a little farther
from the baby you are today.

That thought
it softens me,
and it shatters me.

So I watch you
with wide, quiet eyes.
I trace your moments
like constellations I'll never forget.
Because I know
this is fleeting.

But here's the grace:
though you won't stay little,
though I can't rewind or pause,
motherhood lingers
etched into my soul,
forever mine,
forever yours.

25. Let me love you

Let me love
the darkest parts of you.
Not just the light
but the ache,
the shadows,
the stories you whisper only in silence.

Show me your scars,
not to explain them,
but so I may kiss them
once for the pain,
twice for the strength.

Take me to the walls
you've built around your heart.
The ones no one sees,
the ones you hide behind.

We won't tear them down.
We'll carve soft cracks,
just wide enough
for light to slip through.

And there,

in that quiet space,
we'll dance.

We'll plant seeds
in the soil of your past,
water them with laughter,
and grow something new.

You don't have to be perfect.
Just present.
Just real.
And I...
I will stay.

26. Together but not in love

Isn't it heartbreaking
how many are in love,
but never together?

How many sit side by side,
yet feel miles apart?
We hold hands with those
who never hold our hearts,
speak soft words
to ears that never truly hear.

We walk beside warm bodies
that feel like shadows,
laugh in rooms echoing
with quiet ache.
Eyes meet
but souls miss each other
in the in-between.

So many goodbyes
without ever leaving,
so many hellos
without arriving.

Love exists,
but so often
not where we are.

27. The ones who stay

As you grow, the truth is clear,
Not all who come will stay near.
The circle shrinks, but that's okay
The real ones never drift away.

The bar gets high, the heart gets wise,
You see through charm and perfect lies.
No time for games or empty talk,
You want true hearts who walk your walk.

You learn to guard your sacred space,
To value peace, not just a face.
It's not how many call your name,
But who would love you just the same.

The ones who show up when you fall,
Who see your mess and still stand tall.
Who lift you up, not drain you dry,
And never need a reason why.

They cheer your wins, respect your pain,
They don't compete, compare, or strain.
They let you grow, they give you room,
They light your life, not bring you gloom.

So hold them close, these rarest few,
The hearts so steady, kind, and true.
For in this life, come what may
They're the ones who choose to stay.

28. Here's to the mother

Here's to the mother
the quiet magician
behind birthday candles and Christmas lights,
the one still wrapping gifts
long after midnight,
so her children wake
to wonder.

Here's to the mother
keeper of traditions,
weaver of old tales and new rituals,
the voice that brings bedtime stories to life,
the fearless guardian
against closet monsters
and midnight fears.

Here's to the mother
the healer of wounds
both seen and secret.
With kisses for scraped knees,
and arms wide enough
to hold a broken heart
until it beats steady again.

Here's to the mother
the calm in the chaos,
making messes feel like magic,
turning noise into music,
and never letting the world
see how heavy her cape truly is.

Here's to the mother
last to sleep,
first to rise,
the unshakable center,
the silent strength,
the love that holds
everything together.

29. The way he cares

It doesn't come with flowers,
or loud declarations.
It comes in a quiet voice,
soft with worry,
sharp with love
"Why aren't you taking care of yourself?"

It's not judgment.
It's knowing.
Knowing your silences,
your stubborn strength,
your habit of giving too much
and resting too little.

They see the tired in your eyes
before you do.
They hear the weight in your laugh.
And so they scold
not to hurt,
but to hold you
in the only way you'd let them.

Because real care
isn't always wrapped in comfort.

Sometimes,
it shows up as tough love,
spoken by someone
who refuses to watch you fall apart.

That kind of love
a best friend's kind
is rare.
It's sacred.

And when you hear it,
really hear it,
you realize:
this is what it means
to be truly seen.

30. Wind and stars

If I could keep you little forever,
I wouldn't.
As much as you are a part of me,
you were never mine to keep.

You belong to the wind,
wild and free.
To the moon that will pull your tides,
to the stars that will guide your dreams.

Your laughter holds magic,
your heart holds light
a light this world needs.

You will grow,
you will soar,
you will change everything you touch
in ways only you can.

And if I'm lucky
oh, if I'm lucky
I will be here,
standing quietly in the wings,

watching you become
everything you were meant to be.

31. Worth the wait

She waited
not for noise,
not for grand gestures or perfect words,
but for silence.

A silence that felt full,
not empty.
A presence that wrapped around her
like calm after a storm.

She spent years
giving pieces of herself
to those who never saw the whole.
Years wondering
if love meant shrinking
to be held.

But then
he came.

And beside him,
she found the kind of quiet
that speaks louder than sound.
No need to explain,

no need to impress
just being
was enough.

In his gaze,
she felt wanted.
In his stillness,
appreciated.
In his arms,
utterly adored.

And in that soft, golden moment,
she smiled.
Because now, she knew
why it had taken so long.
Why every lonely night
had led to this.

It was worth the wait.
Every second of it.

32. A love between lifetimes

If I see you in the next life,
no pain, no past, no old strife.
We'll laugh and drink the night away,
and talk of love that slipped astray.

Cold coffee in our favorite cups,
finding Easter eggs and laughing hiccups.
Ice cream melting in summer heat,
sticky hands and hearts that beat.

In winters, we'll get warm and close,
wrapped in blankets, cheeks like rose.
No rush, no rules, just you and me,
in a world where we were meant to be.

Not this life, we missed our cue,
but maybe the next, I'll end with you.
Where timing's kind and stars align,
and what we lost becomes divine.

33. Your coffee order

Be with the one who knows your brew,
The swirl, the strength, the sugar too.
Who orders first, without a glance,
Because he knows, not just by chance.

He's not just someone passing through,
He knows the quiet sides of you.
He waits for you in café light,
And makes the ordinary feel just right.

He finds new spots you've never been,
And makes each latte feel like sin.
Not just a friend, not just a phase,
He's someone who will always stay.

The one who knows your coffee blend,
Is not a crush that time will end.
He's the real one, soft and true
The kind of love that knows all of you.

34. You're my copyright

Dear Best Friend,

I saw you being real cute today
laughing, flirting, giving them your yay.
And for a second, I had to pause,
like... should I call my lawyer, or just applaud?

Let me remind you, sweet and clear:
you didn't get this fabulous alone, my dear.
I've been here—through drama, coffee, and doom
so don't act brand new when you walk in a room.

You can mingle, sparkle, make the world swoon,
but don't forget who taught you to glow like the moon.
Your heart? Trademarked.
That laugh? Patented too.
And bestie, let's be real
your best moments include me, not who?

So go on, be friendly and have your little chats,
but remember who owns the rights to all that.

35. You were there, too

Some days,
I wander back
to where it all began
the place where your smile
first met my heart.

I sit with the ghosts
of our laughter,
rewinding time
like an old song
I still know by heart.

I replay the memories,
soft and slow,
just to remind myself
it wasn't just a dream.
It wasn't all in my head.

You were there, too.
Weren't you?

36. I wish you roses

I cannot wish you happiness
without breaking my own heart
to see you bloom in fields
where I must stand apart.

So I won't whisper joy
that leaves me in the cold,
nor offer up my peace
for a story left untold.

But still
I wish you roses,
soft and crimson bright,
may they bloom beneath your footsteps
and kiss you in the light.

I hope you grow,
through every storm and flame,
even if I'm not the hand
that helps you find your name.

Love does not always follow,
but it sometimes lets you go

and in that letting,
still can hope you grow.

37. You're my home

Don't ask me where you stand with me,
Or how important you might be.
You're not a line I check or place
You're comfort, light, and warm embrace.

You are my *home*, my heart's safe space,
A steady calm, a soft embrace.
Not made of walls or bricks or beams
But built from laughter, love, and dreams.

When life feels heavy, loud, or wrong,
You are my quiet, my sweetest song.
You've held my heart in hands so true,
And never asked for more than you.

So if you doubt, or start to fear
Just close your eyes, and feel me near.
You're not just part of what I do
My world begins and ends with *you*.

With all the love I never say,
Me

38. Then and now

Then:
Every morning bloomed with your words,
sunlight spilling through a screen
soft hellos that kissed my heart,
a comfort quiet and unseen.

Each night, your voice would close the day,
like lullabies wrapped in a call,
and sleep came easy, wrapped in warmth
I never feared the fall.

Now:
My day begins with fragile hope,
a whisper that you might appear,
but hours pass like silent ghosts,
and dusk returns with tears.

The echo of you haunts my time,
in empty spaces you once filled
a rhythm lost, a pulse gone quiet,
a heart unwilling to be stilled.

39. Permission to mourn

The worst part of missing you
was never the ache in my chest
but the silence that followed,
the doubt that clung to my breath.

I didn't know if I was allowed to.
You were never really mine
just a fleeting maybe,
a shadow in the corner of time.

Still, I held you in quiet ways,
between the lines I never spoke,
in glances that begged for meaning,
in dreams that vanished with smoke.

Is it okay if I cry for you now,
though the world never saw us begin?
Can I grieve what was never whole,
a love that lived only within?

Because even unspoken hearts can break,
and even near-strangers leave scars
and I'm still stitching my soul back together,
alone, beneath borrowed stars.

40. Never let go

I loved him like a child might do,
With something warm and soft and true.
Like teddy bears or worn-out charms,
I found my peace within his arms.

He was the calm in all my days,
A light that cut through cloudy haze.
I held him close, my safest place,
With sleepy eyes and full embrace.

No reason why, I just knew so
He felt like home, I couldn't let go.
He was my comfort, heart and soul,
The missing piece that made me whole.

And though the world may change and grow,
Some loves stay small and never let go.

41. If the universe had said yes

Sometimes,
it's not you I miss,
but the echo
of a life we never lived
the mornings we never woke to,
the hands we never aged with.

I don't ache for your presence
so much as the promise
the whispered dreams
we built like stars,
thinking fate would align
just because we dared to believe.

I mourn the quiet maybes,
the almosts and not-quites,
the love that bloomed
but never rooted
deep enough to stay.

If the universe had said yes
just once,
just softly

we might have had
forevers written in skin,
in laughter,
in shared skies.

But it didn't.
And so I grieve
not for you,
but for the beautiful life
we never got to meet.

42. My mom was my home

One day, my child will speak
of love not just in words,
but in the warmth that lived
between quiet moments
and gentle hands.

She will tell someone
what home felt like
and I won't be a place
with walls and windows,
but the arms that held her
when the world felt too big.

I hope she says,
"My mom was my home."
That I was the calm
in her storms,
the light she looked for
in the dark.

That I made her feel
safe in her skin,
seen in her silence,
loved without question

not for what she did,
but simply for being.

I hope she remembers
a voice that softened pain,
a presence that never wavered,
a heart that chose her
every single day.

Because more than anything,
I want her to carry this truth:
she always belonged,
and she was always enough
in the place
where love first began.

43. Worth some kind of poetry

We made love in silence,
not a word between us
just breath,
just heartbeats
syncing like verses
in a poem only we could write.

Our lips,
still wet from our favorite songs,
tasted like memories
warm, familiar,
dripping with melody and meaning.

The world fell away,
no noise, no time,
just the hush between notes
and the way your fingers
spoke fluently in touch.

If this isn't poetry
the way we moved,
the way we became
a language of skin and sound

then nothing ever was.

Because loving you
in the silence,
with music still dancing
on our mouths,
has to be worth
some kind of forever.

44. How can I delete you?

I can delete your photograph,
Erase our smiles, our frozen laugh.
I'll swipe away that captured face,
But not the warmth, the sweet embrace.

I can erase the words you wrote,
Each loving line, each heartfelt note.
I'll clear the screen, pretend it's through
But screens don't hold the soul of you.

I'll block your number, shut the door,
Pretend we never were before.
But silence only makes it worse
Your name still lingers in each verse.

Your face still dances in my mind,
In every crowd, it's you I find.
Your voice still hums in every song,
A melody where you belong.

And memories? They won't delete.
They rise like tides, they taste so sweet.
They burn like stars I can't outrun
A love that's lost, but never done.

You're gone in ways the world can see,
But still so deep inside of me.
No code, no key, no great escape
From love that time cannot reshape.

45. I still check on you

Even after all this time,
when your name no longer lives
on my lips,
I still find myself
checking in on you
quietly, secretly,
like a prayer I never stopped whispering.

You look happy now.
And I hope you are.
God, I hope you are.
Not just in the way photos smile,
but in the way your soul exhales
peaceful, full,
finally free.

It's strange, isn't it?
How someone can stop being yours,
but never really stop being home.
I don't long for us the way I once did,
but I still carry the shape of you
in the softest corners of me.

I don't reach out.

I don't expect anything.
But still
on quiet nights,
in passing scrolls,
you appear.
And I ache.

Not for what was,
but for what could've been
if timing had been kinder,
if hearts had been braver,
if the stars had only said yes.

Some loves don't get an ending.
They just live on,
gently,
in the spaces between moving on
and never forgetting.

And maybe that's what love really is
not something that fades,
but something that stays,
quiet and beautiful,
even when it's no longer ours.

46. The day I chose ME

I didn't walk away
because I stopped loving you.
God, I loved you
with everything I had,
even the pieces of me
I should've kept for myself.

I walked away
because loving you
meant losing me.
And somewhere along the way,
I realized
I was disappearing
in the name of holding on.

You didn't have to be cruel
neglect can be quiet.
It hides in the way you never asked,
never saw,
never reached back
when I was breaking
just to stay close.

I begged the universe for you.

But eventually,
I stopped waiting
for a version of you
that would never arrive.

It's not selfish
to choose peace
over pain dressed as passion.
It's not selfish
to stop bleeding
for someone who never noticed the wounds.

I walked away
because I finally heard the voice inside me
say,
"Enough."

I walked away
because I learned
what love is supposed to feel like
and it wasn't this.

So no
I didn't stop loving you.
I just started loving me.
And for the first time,
that was enough.

47. A thousand times more

In the quiet of memory,
I return to you
to the warmth of your laughter,
the way your presence filled a room
without a single word.

If I had known
those moments were borrowed from forever,
I would have slowed the sun,
begged the stars to wait,
held back the turning of the earth
just to stay within your light
a little longer.

I would have said "I love you"
a thousand times more
in every breath,
in every glance,
in every silent moment
when my heart knew,
but my voice was too quiet.

I would have held you closer,
so close that time itself

might have paused
to witness love
wrapped in something
so beautifully human,
so achingly divine.

But time,
that thief dressed in ordinary days,
carried you forward
while I stayed behind
with arms still reaching
and words still blooming
on my tongue.

Yet even now,
in the hush between heartbeats,
I say it still
I love you.
For every moment I missed,
for every second I'd give back the world to feel again
I love you
a thousand times more.

48. Rich in love

I look around at what I've made
small hands in mine, soft laughter near,
a home built not of gold or stone,
but tender hearts that hold me dear.

The walls may not be lined with wealth,
no diamonds gleam, no fortune grand,
but joy lives in the little things
a crayon drawing, a reaching hand.

Their sleepy smiles, their evening hugs,
the way they call me when they fall,
remind me that I'm rich beyond
what banks could ever count at all.

I may not wear a crown of coin,
no stocks, no treasures stored away,
but love pours in like morning sun
and brightens every single day.

This life I've built, this sacred gift,
these souls that chose to call me "mine"
it's more than perfect, more than luck,
it's something rare, and pure, divine.

So measure me not by what I own,
but by the love that fills this space
for I am rich in every way
that time and money can't replace.

49. A dream come true

We once saw her in a dream,
A little girl in sunlight's gleam.
Chasing butterflies through skies so blue,
Running like the wind, the morning dew.

Tiny feet on grassy ground,
Laughter like the softest sound.
Eyes that sparkled, pure and bright,
A glimpse of love in golden light.

She was magic, soft and small,
The sweetest dream we could recall.
And then one day, the dream came true
She came to life, and came to you.

Now in our home, her laughter rings,
She dances, twirls, and brightly sings.
No longer just a dream we knew,
She's here.. our miracle, brand new.

She made us parents with her grace,
Put light and love in every space.
And every day, we see it clear
That dream we held is living here.

50. Love is the foundation

Marriage isn't something that runs on its own,
it's not a flame that never needs tending.
It's a garden that grows with gentle care,
a choice we keep making,
not just a beginning.

In the rush of mornings,
amid cries and spilled milk,
in the lullaby hush of midnight tears,
we must still see each other
not just parents, not just partners,
but soulmates through the years.

Date your love,
even when you're tired.
Reach for their hand
when the world feels too loud.
Make them your haven,
your soft place to land,
when everything else is a crowd.

Because children grow,
and one day the toys are packed away.
Friends will come and go

like seasons that cannot stay.
But you two
you are the constant thread,
woven through the fabric of each day.

When everything changes,
when time wears new lines on your face,
let your love be the steady light,
the home,
the sacred place.

Not perfect,
but patient.
Not flawless,
but true.
A bond built not just in the big moments
but in the quiet choosing
of me and you.

51. The light of my morning

Each morning the sun dares to rise,
but it is not the dawn that stirs my soul
it is you.
That tiny breath, that peaceful face,
a masterpiece only heaven could have shaped.

Your lashes kiss your cheeks like whispers,
your hand, so small, rests near mine
as if reminding me
this is love,
this is purpose.

The world may spin with noise and need,
but in that quiet moment,
when I wake to you,
time softens.
Everything becomes still,
holy,
right.

You are the miracle I never knew to pray for,
the joy stitched into my ordinary days,
the gentle reason my heart
beats softer,

sings louder,
and hopes endlessly.

Any day I wake to your beautiful little face
is a good day
no...
it is the best kind of day.

52. She doesn't know it yet

She doesn't know it yet, my dear,
How just her breath could draw me near
How in my silence, lost and gray,
Her tiny light lit up the way.

No guiding star, no healing word,
Could touch me like her laughter stirred.
She came so small, yet somehow strong,
And taught my weary heart its song.

When nights were heavy, hope ran thin,
She placed her warmth beneath my skin.
A whisper in the darkest part
My daughter, keeper of my heart.

She doesn't know she saved me then,
But one day, when she's older, when
She wonders what she means to me,
I'll tell her: *She helped set me free.*

53. A simple life, with you

The dream was never gold or grand,
Not mansions high or foreign land
Just waking where your laughter stays,
In burnt toast mornings, soft sunrays.

We'd count the coins, the rent half due,
But find the wealth in loving true;
Long days would end with tangled grace,
As moonlight danced upon your face.

No silken thread, no diamond bright,
Could match your hoodie wrapped so tight
The way your voice, though tired and low,
Still tells me all I need to know.

Through storms and silence, hand in hand,
We'll build a world, not big but planned;
A life of effort, stitched with care
A simple love, beyond compare.

54. Always, for you

Never hesitate, my child, to say,
"Mom, I'm not okay,"
For your voice will break through any storm
That shadows my own day.

Though I may carry silent cracks,
And burdens deep and wide,
I'd lay them down without a thought
To sit here by your side.

No sorrow in your gentle heart
Could ever scare me far;
I'd gather every falling star
To show you who you are.

So come to me with tear-stained eyes,
With trembling words and pain
I'll hold you through the darkest hours
Until you smile again.

For no matter how the world may turn,
Or how broken I may be,
You will always find me waiting

Forever here.

For thee.

55. Could I? Maybe

Could I but speak the aching of my soul,
When you were near, and silence veiled my heart,
I would have whispered love to make you whole,
And sworn no fate could tear our lives apart.

A thousand times, my lips betrayed my will
They trembled, mute, though fire burned within;
Your gaze, your breath, the hush when all was still
Each moment begged for love I held too thin.

I should have drawn you closer, let you stay,
And in your arms, made war with fleeting time;
Each heartbeat cried to hold the night at bay,
Each touch, a prayer half-formed, half lost in rhyme.

Now memory is all I dare embrace
Your ghost lives softly in the silent space.

56. Unnamed

The world called us lovers,
But we never knew the name
We walked through days as shadows
Of a fire without flame.

We laughed in quiet corners,
Our silence softly spoke,
But never dared to wonder
If hearts were gently broke.

We thought it was just friendship,
A closeness undefined,
While every touch, unspoken,
Was poetry in kind.

We behaved like secret lovers
Eyes lingering too long,
Fingers brushing meanings
Where only friends belong.

Yet when the world saw magic,
We claimed it wasn't true.
They called us love
But we only ever knew

The ache of almost
And the beauty of not quite.

57. Midnight almosts

They were never defined, no title, no claim,
Just midnight confessions and playing love's game.
She'd watch for his light in the silence of night,
He'd wait for her name in the soft morning light.

They laughed in the dark where the world couldn't see,
Shared secrets like stars scattered over the sea.
He'd call her "trouble," she'd call him "fool,"
But silence between them broke every rule.

One night she asked with a tremble, a sigh,
"What are we?" beneath a half-honest sky.
He said, *"Something beautiful... just not today."*
She smiled through the ache, let the dream slip away.

Now they are strangers who almost had more,
Two hearts that knocked but stayed at the door.
Not lovers, not friends, just a nearly missed spark
A love left unfinished in the quiet and dark.

58. Only him

What if he leaves? they ask me, low
Then I'll wait, I whisper, soft and slow.
Through seasons that change and skies that fall,
My love will linger, through it all.

What if he forgets you? comes the doubt.
Then I'll remind him, without a shout.
With echoes of laughter, memories spun,
In the quiet corners where we were one.

What if he loves another face?
Then I'll love him still, from a silent place.
No need to hold, no need to near,
Love doesn't vanish when hearts disappear.

So yes, I'll love him, come what may
In dreams, in dust, in light, in grey.
Not just today, but endlessly,
Only him, in every reality.

59. Beneath the city lights

He was lost in thought, heavy with night,
So she took her away, beneath city lights.
No words were needed, just silence and sound,
As they drove through the quiet, the world spinning
round.

She stopped the car, turned, took his hand,
"You don't have to speak, I just want to stand."
And in that moment, with nothing to say,
He found all she needed, in her quiet stay.

60. My one sided heart

What's your favorite place? they ask with a smile.
His arms, she replies, *I'd rest there awhile.*
No map could lead to a haven so true,
Where silence speaks, and the world feels new.

And your favorite sound? they gently implore.
His laugh, she says, *I could crave nothing more.*
It dances like rain on a windowpane,
Soft and sweet, yet stitched with pain.

Your favorite time? they ask, leaning in.
When he looks at me, she says with a grin.
For in his eyes, the whole sky glows,
Even if he'll never know.

So he's your everything? No, she sighs,
He's more—he's my truth in every disguise.
Your boyfriend, then? No, she says, torn apart,
He's my best friend... and my one-sided heart.

61. I never stopped wanting to

Her phone rang once, then quiet took hold,
She gazed at the name that once made her whole
A name she hadn't seen for far too long,
The one she whispered to the stars in her song.

A missed call—just one—her heart raced anew,
She typed, *"Are you okay?"* as hope softly grew.
Three dots flickered, then disappeared fast,
Her pulse was a drumbeat, tied to the past.

Then, finally, his words came tender and slow,
*"I just wanted to hear your voice, but I was scared you'd
let me go."*
Her fingers trembled as she typed her reply,
*"I never stopped wanting to... even when I had to say
goodbye.*

62. Only for her

If she is heaven, he'd long to fly,
To rest in her light, to never say goodbye.
If she is tears, he'd weep with grace,
Each drop a testament to her embrace.

If she is pain, he'd welcome the hurt,
A love so deep, it aches in the dirt.
If she is the moon, he'd be the star,
Shining beside her, no distance too far.

If she is the ocean, he'd be the wave,
Endlessly crashing, eternally brave.
If she is winter, he'd be the fire,
The warmth she needs, her one desire.

Only for her, he'd give all he'd know,
For in her love, he'd always grow.

63. A mother's wish

If I could give my daughter one thing,
It would be the strength to always sing
To trust her voice when the world gets loud,
To stand her ground and stand so proud.

To walk away when she feels small,
To leave behind what doesn't call,
To never stay in spaces tight,
That ask her to give up her light.

To know her worth is not a prize,
Not tied to looks or others' eyes.
That love should feel both kind and safe,
A steady hand, a warm embrace.

I hope she grows up sure and free,
Never doubting what she's meant to be.
For the world will try to pull her down,
But I won't always be around.

Yet in her heart, she'll always know,
Her worth is hers, and hers to show.

64. A distant dream

Brain said, "*He loves someone new,*
You never had a chance, it's true."
Heart replied, with gentle grace,
"*But don't we love the moon's soft face?*

We know it's distant, far away,
Yet still, we watch it night and day.
Sometimes, love is just the same
A light we see, but cannot claim.

65. A love like this

Don't lose him," her sister said,
With knowing eyes and a gentle head.
"*Why?*" she asked, a little shy,
Not quite sure the reason why.

Her sister smiled, soft and true,
"*The way he always looks at you*
It's just like Dad with Mom, you see,
Like love was meant to always be."

She held those words, close and near,
A quiet truth she longed to hear.
For in his eyes, she now could find
A love that's deep, forever kind.

66. Blushing into forever

This is our last video call," he said,
"No more late-night chats ahead."
She laughed, her cheeks a rosy hue,
"Stop being dramatic—it's me and you."

"Tomorrow's here, the wait is done,
We'll wake up under the same sun."
No more screens, no calls, no delay,
Just holding hands at break of day.

He smiled wide, his heart at peace,
As all the distance found its release.
Love had waited, now it would stay
Together, forever, starting today.

67. A cup and a smile

He never said the words out loud,
But showed them in the morning crowd.
Each day, a coffee on her desk,
A quiet gift, a sweet request.

Then one day, tucked beneath her cup,
A little note was folded up:
*"For the girl who makes each Monday bright,
Who turns the gray to morning light."*

She smiled, heart warm with surprise,
A quiet joy behind her eyes.
Next morning, on his desk she placed
A coffee too, with quiet grace.

Her note was simple, soft, and true:
"For the boy who makes skies blue."

He looked up fast, caught off guard,
To find her there, not very far.
She smiled at him, her eyes aglow
The start of something sweet and slow.

68. Stolen sips

Each morning started just the same,
Her coffee gone, it felt like a game.
Vanilla latte, smooth and light,
No sugar added, her daily delight.

She left a note, annoyed and clear:
"To whoever keeps taking it—buy your own, dear."
A small complaint, a simple plea,
To let her morning coffee be.

But the next day, to her surprise,
A note appeared before her eyes:
"I would, but yours tastes better still
It warms me more than any will."

She looked around, her heartbeat quick,
Then saw him smirking, calm and slick.
He held her cup, the guilty grin
The playful thief she'd never seen.

The coffee loss, she didn't mind,
For something sweeter she might find.

69. The dream he held

He dreamt of her before she came,
A tiny soul, a whispered name.
A baby girl, his heart's own light,
A piece of him, so pure, so right.

He saw her clearly in his dreams
Big shining eyes, soft lips that gleam.
Brown hair like Mommy's, flowing sweet,
A little world beneath his feet.

He wished with every breath he had,
For love, for life, for joy unclad.
He pictured her, so crystal true,
As if his heart already knew.

A daddy's dupe, the world would say,
A perfect echo made from clay.
He spoke to stars, he prayed so deep,
And held her image in his sleep.

And then one day, his dream was real,
A tiny hand he'd longed to feel.
She wrapped his finger, soft and tight,
And smiled at him with all her might.

Those twinkling eyes, that perfect face,
The universe fell into place.
She was his song, his breath, his prayer,
A love so vast, beyond compare.

He held her close, he kissed her head,
And silent thanks to God he said.
No greater gift, no deeper part,
Than this small girl who owned his heart.

A princess born from dream and grace,
His soul reborn in her small face.

And every beat his heart now knew,
Whispered:
"*You, my love... are dreams come true.*"

70. The love they couldn't keep

They weren't allowed to love out loud,
Not in the open, not in the crowd.
So they met in glances held too long,
In casual talks, in half-spun songs.

The world would never understand,
Their hearts were tied to different plans.
Promises lived in other hands,
And time slipped through like falling sand.

But when their eyes would find their way,
The universe forgot the day.
And in that pause, in stolen skies,
A secret garden bloomed inside.

They never touched, they never spoke,
Yet in each goodbye, something broke.
A mourning for what couldn't be,
A love the world would never see.

Was it love?
Yes, pure and deep.
The kind that silence swears to keep.

The kind that aches where words can't go,
A love impossible, yet whole.

71. My safe place

He kissed her forehead, soft and slow,
And whispered, "*You're safe, you know.*"
She smiled, not seeing in his eyes,
The quiet storms he'd kept disguised.

She thought he gave her all his grace,
Not knowing she became his place.
For in her arms, he found release
A home, a heart, a kind of peace.

She felt protected, held, and free,
But he..
he finally felt safe to be.

72. That special night

The night was soft, the stars were kind,
She left her fears far behind.
Once shy to give her all away,
Now love and trust had found their way.

In his arms, the world was right,
She melted into him that night.
Each kiss, each touch, a whispered fire,
Awakening her deep desire.

Goosebumps rose with every sigh,
As love lit sparks across the sky.
No fear remained, no walls, no fight
Just two souls dancing in the night.

His hands wrote poems on her skin,
Each tender touch pulled her within.
She gave him all, her heart, her breath,
A love that dared to conquer death.

And when the morning light was born,
She wore his love like jewels, like dawn.
Soft marks of passion, sweet and true,
A quiet proof their hearts once knew.

She woke more beautiful, more bright,
A woman crowned by love that night.

73. A whole universe

You are not a backup plan,
Not a pause between lost hands.
Not a "maybe" in a restless mind,
Not a space they leave behind.

You are a whole universe,
Woven in stars and endless verse.
Meant to be felt with trembling hands,
Not touched only when time demands.

You are not a shelter for the rain,
Not a name they call in vain.
You are the story, the dream, the flight
The steady flame in the quiet night.

You were never meant for convenience,
But for wonder, for deep believing.
A soul to be met with open skies
Not a passing thought,
But a rising tide.

74. Sitting here, loving you

I am sitting here,
dreaming of the moment when the distance fades,
when I can finally fall into your arms
and hear the sound of your heartbeat beneath my ear.

I am sitting here,
waiting for the warmth of your hand in mine,
for the way our fingers will fit
as if they were always meant to find each other.

I am sitting here,
remembering your gentle touch,
the way it brushed away the world,
leaving only you, only us.

I am sitting here,
picturing your eyes
the ones that see me clearer than anyone ever has,
your smile
the one that makes every heavy thing inside me
disappear.

I am sitting here,
falling in love with you a thousand times over,

in every breath, in every heartbeat,
in every silent prayer whispered to the stars.

I am sitting here,
loving you more with every second,
longing for the day when sitting here
becomes standing there
in front of you,
hand in hand,
heart to heart,
finally home.

75. The love you left in me

You taught me how to love again,
To heal, to hope, to trust the rain.
You showed me dreams don't have to stay,
That endings come, and that's okay.
Not every heart that's meant to roam
Will take you with it when it's home.
But love, you said, still leaves its light
A flame that warms the coldest night.

You taught me love is not a race,
Not something one must chase or chase.
It's giving all, it's standing near,
It's loving deep without the fear.
You taught me loss can hold a grace,
That parting hands still leave a trace
A mark that time cannot erase,
A tender, silent, sacred place.

You freed me from the past I wore,
Unlocked a heart that asked for more.
You taught me faith, you taught me peace,
You gave me back my own release.
You showed me love is not a chain,
But something born through joy and pain.

You taught me love is letting go,
And trusting what we'll never know.

Now everywhere I go, you stay
In softer smiles, in lighter days.
In every crack, in every seam,
You are the root beneath my dreams.
I love the soul you helped me see
The fearless, braver part of me.
Though life may shift, though seasons flee,
You are the love that set me free.

76. Choosing forever

There's no purpose in dating
if forever isn't somewhere in your mind.
At first, it all feels like magic
the late-night talks,
the endless texts,
the butterflies fluttering just right.

But that isn't love.
That's wonder
sweet, fleeting,
beautiful, but passing.

Because love begins
when the spark fades,
when laughter quiets into silence,
when surprise turns into routine.
That's when hearts are tested,
and choice begins to matter.

Love is not how loudly it starts,
but how gently it stays.
Not in how it thrills,
but in how it endures.

Most run from that risk
the unknown,
the promise without proof.
They chase comfort,
mistake warmth for forever,
and call temporary things home.

But every bond faces its truth
it either deepens into always,
or it ends,
leaving behind the echo
of time not truly honored.

Forever is frightening,
because it asks for faith
in what cannot be seen.
You might change.
They might too.
The world will shift beneath your feet.

And yet,
love still whispers
step forward,
risk the unknown,
and choose.

Again and again,
choose.

77. The one who sees me

To the person who sees my worth
even when I forget my own
thank you.

You've been my voice
when mine trembled in silence,
my strength
when I had none left to give.

You've lifted me in ways
the world will never see,
loved me not for who I try to be,
but for who I truly am.

You've given me reason
to celebrate this life
and in you,
I found my greatest gift of all,
our daughter
a living piece of our love.

You've trusted me,
believed in me,
stood beside me

through every rise and fall.

You are my calm,
my heart,
my home in human form.

Thank you, my love,
for seeing me,
for choosing me,
for being my forever strength.

78. My only goal

My greatest dream, my truest role,
is simple, to be a mom with soul.
To guide her heart, so pure, so kind,
to leave all cruelty far behind.

To teach her strength when days grow rough,
to show that love will be enough.
To help her rise when she may fall,
and face the world, standing tall.

To teach her grace where anger grows,
to bloom with light the darkness knows.
To be her calm, her gentle cheer,
the voice that whispers, *"I'm right here."*

If she learns courage, heart, and grace,
and wears compassion on her face,
then I've fulfilled my deepest role
to be a good mom. My only goal.

79. My why

The world sees a little girl
so small, so innocent,
with laughter that dances through the air.

But I see so much more.
I see my reason to breathe,
my why,
the piece of my soul
that decided to live outside my body.

When she whispers *"Mumma,"*
the world stops
every ache, every worry,
melts into that one word.

When she wraps her tiny arms around me,
I feel whole again.
As if every crack in my heart
was made only to be filled by her love.

She is my calm after every storm,
my light when the days feel dim,
my purpose written in flesh and heartbeat.

She's not just my little girl
she's my forever person,
my reason,
my home.

80. The second time

It isn't the same anymore
and maybe that's the beauty of it.

We once met too early,
hearts full of feelings
we didn't know how to name.
We pushed without meaning to,
we hid behind walls
we thought would keep us safe.

Love wasn't lost because it was wrong
only because we weren't ready
to hold it right.

So life separated us,
taught us lessons we never asked for:
how to stand alone,
how to stop searching for someone
to glue our broken pieces together.

And somewhere between letting go
and learning to heal,
we grew into the people
our love needed all along.

Now, if we return
it isn't for comfort,
or because we need saving.
It's because we *choose* to come back.

We know the ache
of a world without each other.
We move slower now,
with steadier hands
and softer hearts.

Sometimes, we must fall apart
to understand how to come back whole.

The love we rebuild
won't erase the past
but it will *survive* it.

It isn't about holding tight
it's about holding *well.*

And maybe, just maybe
the second time
is the only time
we truly get it right.

81. That one friend

Someone once asked me,
"Why are you always with that one friend?"
And I smiled
because how do you explain comfort?

It's the quiet kind of magic,
where words aren't needed,
and silence feels like a soft song.

No pretending, no weight to carry,
just peace breathing between two hearts.

Some friendships don't demand,
they simply exist
like a calm sea beneath the chaos,
like home in human form.

The laughter flows,
the moments linger,
and just *being* is enough.

Such souls are rare
when you find one,
you don't let go.

You hold on gently,
but you hold on *forever.*

82. Bound to this heart

You can never run too far,
Your heart will follow where you are.
Its whispers echo, soft yet deep,
In waking hours, in silent sleep.

You may wander, you may hide,
Cross the seas or shift the tide,
But in the end, you'll come to see
Your heart still holds your destiny.

So pause, and let it softly speak,
Its voice is gentle, wise, unique.
For peace will bloom, and pain depart,
The day you listen to your heart.

83. In between the naps

We've changed, both you and I,
No midnight talks beneath the sky.
Our plans now wait on tiny dreams,
Measured in naps and half-heard screams.

The days rush by, we barely see,
A moment left for you and me.
The "us" we knew feels far, apart
Yet love still lingers, quiet at heart.

Then I see you with our little one,
Your laughter soft, the day half done.
And in that glance, so pure, so true,
I fall in love again.. with you.

84. The softest reminder

This morning, as our baby cried,
I held him close, his tears, my guide.
The world was blurred in sleepless haze,
Another dawn, another maze.

And then, so soft, I almost missed
Your hand found mine, a fleeting kiss.
A touch that spoke, without a sound,
Of love still quietly all around.

No words were said, yet I could hear,
"I see you, love. I'm always near."
In that small moment, tender, true
I felt the world grow calm... through you.

And though the days feel long and wild,
Our hearts still meet in every mile.
Through tired eyes and lullaby's hue,
We're finding love in something new.

85. When love found a name

He drew her close, his touch so light,
The world stood still in soft twilight.
She whispered then, her cheeks aflame,
"What are you doing? Someone might see, love refrain."

But time moved on, as time will do,
Their hearts stayed bound, their world grew too.
Now little feet run through their days,
And love wears gentler, deeper ways.

Again he pulls her, warmth in his eyes,
She laughs and blushes, half in surprise
"What are you doing? Our kids might see."
And in her smile, he finds his peace.

That someone once, now has a name,
In giggles, chaos, love's new flame.
For what began in secret hues,
Now blooms in life they've built, so true.

Their love grew roots, it found its place,
In tiny hands and soft embrace.
For when love finds a name to claim,
It's not the same, yet still the same.

86. When it all began

She finally shared her number one day,
A quiet smile, a shy "okay."
And there he was, in moments few,
Changing pictures, one... then two.

Each snapshot told what words could not,
His sweetest charm, his playful plot.
In five short minutes, a slideshow spun,
Thirty-four faces, but only one won.

She watched, amused, her heart half-stirred,
Then typed a note, her very first word:
"You looked good in all, I must confess
Now if you're done, shall we talk, I guess?"

And just like that, beneath her tease,
Love began with simple ease.
Not grand or loud, no scripted part
Just laughter finding its way to heart.

87. Between him and her

The most beautiful bond beneath the sky,
Is not of lovers, yet hearts that tie.
A girl and a boy, so different, yet near,
They share their souls without any fear.

No promises sworn, no need to pretend,
Just laughter that heals, and hearts that mend.
They care, they tease, they stand side by side,
Through every storm, through every tide.

He wipes her tears when dreams fall apart,
She brings him peace, she steadies his heart.
No hidden wish, no secret plan,
Just pure affection, soul to soul, human to human.

For love wears many forms, my friend,
Not all of them with romance to end.
Sometimes, it's simple, loyal, and grand
A girl and a boy, walking hand in hand.

88. Now I know, Maa

All my life, you used to say,
"One day, you'll know, it's a mother's way."
I'd smile, I'd nod, I'd laugh it through,
Never knowing what you knew.

Those sleepless nights, the gentle care,
The silent prayers whispered in air.
The way you gave, the way you stayed,
The love that never once decayed.

And now, as I cradle my child so near,
Your voice returns, so soft, so clear.
Every heartbeat, every sigh,
Echoes the love that doesn't die.

Now I know, Maa.. your endless grace,
Your tired eyes, your warm embrace.
And in this knowing, pure and true,
I love you more... for all you knew.

89. Call your love home

Call your love back home tonight,
From every shadow, every light.
From every smile that once was yours,
From whispered dreams and open doors.

Call back the laughter you once gave,
The gentle strength that made hearts brave.
The touch, the warmth, the soft caress
That healed the world with tenderness.

Like a boomerang through skies above,
Let it return, that selfless love.
For all you poured in hearts unknown,
Deserves to rest within your own.

So open wide your waiting heart,
Let your own magic re-ignite.
It's time to feel what you once gave
To love yourself, the way you save.

90. When I'm gone

When I die, don't come too near,
My hands won't wipe away your tear.
The warmth you seek will not remain,
Only silence, only pain.

Remember me in laughter's sound,
In moments where our hearts were bound.
In every hug, in every smile,
Let those stay with you for a while.

Cry if you must, but not too long,
For love still hums its quiet song.
Don't touch the cold that once was me
Hold close the warmth, the memory.

I'd rather live within your heart,
Than see you break, than watch you part.
So let me go, yet keep me near,
In every joy, I'll still be here.

91. Social media love

Social media stole love's slow flame,
Now hearts are restless, never the same.
Endless options blur the view,
What once was deep feels shallow, untrue.

One small fight, a fleeting storm,
And already they seek another form.
Loyalty wanes, patience fades,
Love is lost in virtual charades.

They crave the easy, the picture-perfect scene,
Not the quiet moments, the spaces between.
But love is messy, love takes time,
It grows in hardship, it climbs, it climbs.

Yet all they chase is the glossy show,
Forgetting that true hearts need to grow.
And so real love hides, quiet, unseen,
Buried beneath a digital sheen.

92. Mommy's girl

Everyone speaks of a daddy's girl,
But no one sings of a mommy's world.
She's been mine since love made us one,
Since the very first beat of her tiny drum.

Before she knew my voice, she knew my heart,
Before the world, I was her start.
They say daughters drift as seasons pass,
But we only grow closer, like shadows and grass.

Through sleepless nights and scraped-up knees,
Through whispered secrets and soft-laughed pleas,
We've built a bond that time can't sever,
A love that holds, forever and ever.

One day she'll have her own life, her own place,
Yet I hope she'll always remember this space.
For no matter the years, the highs or the swirl,
She will forever be... my little girl.

93. Marriage in the mess

Your spouse is the one who stays,
Through darkest nights and hardest days.
Who sits beside you when hearts break,
And shares the tears you cannot fake.

They hold your hand through every pain,
Through labor's cry, through loss, through rain.
They may care for you when you can't stand,
Or simply listen, just holding your hand.

Love is not only butterflies or light,
Or candlelit dinners in the quiet night.
It's showing up in grief and mess,
In every storm, in every stress.

Commitment, patience, hearts mature,
Endurance makes a love endure.
For marriage blooms where courage lies
In ugly days and honest skies.

94. Our last coffee date

Our last coffee date, the cup felt cold,
Its bitter taste, a story untold.
Maybe it knew, as we quietly sipped,
That our closeness now would slowly slip.

The café buzzed, but not with cheer,
The familiar peace felt far, unclear.
We smiled politely, played our part,
While shadows whispered in our hearts.

Pretending all was just the same,
Hiding the truth behind our game.
We said goodbye, a fleeting smile,
Knowing this coffee wouldn't last our while.

For love once sweet can slowly fade,
Yet memories linger in the shade.
And though the cups may never meet,
In that bitter warmth, our hearts still beat.

95. She remakes us

We made a tiny human, small and new,
A world of wonder in her eyes so true.
But little did we know, in her gentle ways,
She would reshape our nights and days.

Her laughter mends what time had worn,
Her tears remind us to feel, reborn.
Each tiny hand, each curious glance,
Pulls us deeper into life's dance.

We thought we gave her all we knew,
Yet she gives back more, in ways we never knew.
For in her growth, her love, her art,
She is the one quietly remaking our hearts.

96. Not just a mom

"Just a mom?" you say with doubt,
As if that phrase could figure me out.
Yes, I'm a mom and hear me clear,
I am so much more than it may appear.

I'm alarm clock, cook, and nurse,
A teacher, chauffeur, referee in a hearse.
I'm the handyman, security, and guide,
The photographer who captures pride.

Counselor, hairdresser, planner of days,
ATM, personal assistant, my work never sways.
I chase away monsters, soothe every fear,
My love runs constant, year after year.

No holidays, no sick days, no time to rest,
Day and night, I give my best.
I may be "just a mom" in someone's eyes,
But to my child, I am the sunrise.

So if you're a mom, proud and true,
Repost this love, there's nothing you wouldn't do.
For being a mom is the fiercest art,
A lifetime of giving, straight from the heart.

97. Love in spite

Even if I tell you to go away,
Don't listen, just stubbornly stay.
Even if I say, "don't talk to me,"
Fill the silence with your silly glee.

Even if I mutter, "I hate you,"
Look in my eyes, they'll tell what's true.
For every word I say in spite,
Hides a plea to hold me tight.

Stay when I push, love when I fight,
See through my storm to where I'm right.
For sometimes love, though hard to show,
Is found in the "leave me," that means "don't go."

98. Not an easy girl

I'm not an easy girl, you see,
I shut down when storms come to me.
I pull away when feelings run deep,
And hide the nights I cannot sleep.

I hate the spotlight, I hate the game,
Life's not all sunshine, it's fire and rain.
My heart is heavy, my mind won't rest,
I say the wrong things, yet try my best.

I wear a smile, though pain is near,
I hide my past, I hide my fear.
The walls I've built are not for you,
They keep me whole when I feel untrue.

So if you stay, please understand,
These walls are fragile, yet they withstand.
I'm not easy, but I am real,
And this is the way my heart must heal.

99. Everyday hero

If you ask me of my love, I'd say,
"I love him," in the simplest way.
But dig a little, look inside,
You'll find my best friend there resides.

The one I laugh with, cry with too,
Sit in silence, yet still feel true.
Kindest soul I've ever known,
Hard-working, loyal, love clearly shown.

He moves for family, heart in hand,
Shows up when life doesn't go as planned.
In little moments, in everyday ways,
He loves me deeply, through all my haze.

Even when I'm hard to hold,
His love remains, steadfast, bold.
He lifts me higher, brings out my best,
With him beside me, I am blessed.

So every day I whisper thanks,
For this love that fills my heart's wide banks.
Not just a husband, but a friend so true

My life, my laughter, my skies, my blue.
My everyday Hero.

100. One day, I'll close my eyes

One day, I'll close my eyes for the longest time,
Drifting through the memories of your hand in mine.
I'll wander through the laughter, the quiet, the pain,
Through the echoes of us, through sun and through rain.

One day, I'll close them just to see
Your smile, your voice, your soul next to me.
The world may fade, the hours may blur,
But in that darkness, it's only you I infer.

One day, I'll close my eyes to hope,
To feel your warmth if my heart can cope.
To sense your presence in every fleeting thought,
In every tender moment that time has brought.

One day, I'll close them and won't awake,
If not beside you, for my heart's own sake.
Yet even in the silence where shadows roam,
I'll carry your love, I'll carry you home.

For closings are not endings, they're doors ajar,
A passage to where you never feel far.

And in that quiet, where the world disappears,
I'll meet you again, beyond days and years.

101. From strangers to forever

From strangers, we began, unsure, unknown,
Two souls wandering, learning, alone.
From strangers to friends, laughter took flight,
Moments shared under soft, quiet light.

From friends to best friends, hearts intertwined,
Secrets exchanged, your soul meeting mine.
Through every storm, through joy and tears,
We built a bond stronger than years.

From best friends to spouses, love took its place,
A promise, a journey, a shared embrace.
From spouses to parents, our world grew wide,
Tiny hands in ours, love multiplied.

It's been the best journey, the sweetest ride,
With you always here, right by my side.
Through every change, through every endeavor,
I've loved you, my heart, from then to forever.

102. If I were you

If I were you,
I would admire you all my life
like sunlight tracing every curve of dawn,
like silence worshipping the sound of your breath.

I'd kiss your cheeks while you slept,
softly enough to not wake your dreams,
yet deeply enough to live in them.

I'd dance all night,
my hand lost in yours,
as if time itself had paused to watch us sway.

If I were you,
I'd thank the universe for weaving our souls,
for letting me find forever in your eyes.

I'd manifest each sunrise
with you by my side,
sip every coffee as if it were our first,
and travel to all the places
where my heart already wandered with you.

If I were you,

I'd never let your heart break,
I'd hold it like it was the only truth I knew...

But I'm not you
and that's where the ache begins.

103. Conversation with the moon

One quiet night, I looked up high,
to the lonely keeper of the sky.
Her silver glow brushed through the blue,
and I whispered softly, "I envy you."

"You see my lover while the world sleeps,
you guard his dreams, your promise keeps.
You touch his face with your gentle light,
while I just ache through endless night."

The moon, so calm, began to gleam,
her voice like ripples on a dream.
"My child," she said, "if only you knew,
he spends his days just missing you."

I looked away, my heart undone,
"But you," I said, "see everyone
and him, and all his smiles, his eyes,
you watch his world beneath your skies."

The moon grew soft, her shimmer deep,
"I see his tears before he sleeps.
And in those tears, your name does lie

a prayer, a wish, a silent cry."

I bit my lip and whispered through,
"I still envy the sight of you.
You see all lovers, near and far,
their yearning hearts beneath your star."

The moon sighed slow, her glow turned pale,
"Each night I watch love's tender tale
the longing, the waiting, the words unsaid,
the dreams that haunt the sleepless bed.

But I also remind the hearts that roam,
that even apart, they share one home.
The same vast sky, the same cold hue,
the same soft moonlight bathing two."

She paused, then smiled, both kind and true,
"Don't envy me, dear heart so blue.
For love like yours though far, though strained
is the rarest kind the stars have gained.

He looks at me, but sees your face,
he calls your name in night's embrace.
And though you're not close, not in view,
believe me, child... he belongs to you."

104. To my little one

Be brave, my love, the world is wide,
walk with strength and gentle pride.
Know your worth, let no one sway,
shine your light in your own way.

And when life tests your tender heart,
remember, we're never apart
Mumma and Papa, forever near,
to lift you up, to calm your fear.

Go chase your dreams, both big and small,
stand tall, my girl, through rise and fall.
For even when the skies turn gray,
our love will guide your every way.

105. My happy place

My happy place is us .. so true,
the man who loves in every hue.
Through every season, come what may,
his heart has never walked away.

And the little ones who call me "Mom,"
their giggles are my sweetest calm.
Their laughter dances through these walls,
their tiny footsteps joy that calls.

His hand finds mine in daily storm,
his touch, my shelter safe and warm.
And in the chaos, love still flows,
a peace within my heart that grows.

This is the calm I longed to find,
a grace that stills my restless mind.
The family I once prayed would be,
became my world, my melody.

For in their love, I've found my role
the missing piece that made me whole.

106. Still Us

They think we're just Mumma and Papa...
but we're the kids who once fell in love,
two hearts stumbling into forever
without even knowing it.

We built this life with laughter and prayers,
with sleepless nights and hopeful mornings,
with dreams whispered in the dark
and faith stitched into every day.

We're still learning, still growing,
still finding new versions of "us."
And through every season, every storm,
we are still choosing each other
again, and again, and again.

107. My favourite incomplete wish

You're my favourite incomplete wish
the one I hold gently in the dark,
afraid to touch too hard
in case the memory breaks.

So what if we aren't together?
So what if you're the dream
this lifetime refused to honour?
Some loves are carved in silence,
meant only to be felt,
never lived.

I still carry you
in every almost,
every what-if,
every heartbeat that stumbles
when your name drifts through my mind.

But I tell myself there's a life after this,
a place where unfinished love
doesn't have to stay incomplete.
Where souls meet without fear,
where timing can't betray us,

where hearts don't have to choose goodbye.

And there.. in that soft, unseen world
I know I'll find you again.
Not as a dream I couldn't keep,
not as a wish that slipped away,
but as the one wish
that finally, finally
came true.

108. In your embrace

It wasn't just a hug, it was home.
A place where anger melts away,
where tears remember how to stop,
where the whole world falls quiet
for just a heartbeat.

You don't plan it,
you don't speak,
you simply open your arms
and somehow, they always know.

They run to you
like you're gravity,
like their little universe
begins and ends
in the circle of your hold.

And in that moment,
nothing else matters
not the mess,
not the noise,
not the ache of exhaustion
that lingers in your bones.

Because that hug
whispers everything
your heart could ever say:
I see you.
I'm here.
You're safe.

109. Woven into him

He thinks I'm just his wife...
but I'm the keeper of the little moments
he's long forgotten
the dreams he whispered at midnight,
the fears he buried behind a smile,
the strength he didn't know he had.

I'm the witness to his becoming
every stumble, every triumph,
every softening and every storm.
I've loved him through the versions
he didn't even recognize in himself.

He thinks I'm just his wife...
but I carry his laughter in my chest,
his heartbreak in my hands,
his past in my memories
and his future in my prayers.

I'm the one who stayed,
who believed,
who loved him gently
even on the days he couldn't love himself.

If only he knew
I'm not just beside him.
I'm woven into him.

110. The journey of us

We were just two kids in love once
wide-eyed, unsure, dreaming louder than we lived.
Back then, love felt simple...
like stolen moments, whispered promises,
and hearts that didn't know their own strength.

Now we're partners.
Parents.
Teammates in the mess and the magic
building a life out of chaos,
holding each other through the tired days,
laughing through the beautiful ones,
growing in ways our younger selves
could never have imagined.

And every single day,
I thank God for this journey
that the boy I fell for
became the man I get to grow old with.
A love that didn't just last...
it grew up with us.

111. The leftover love

What does heartbreak feel like?
It's that tiny tremble in your stomach
that grows into something you can't name,
the sudden rush in your chest
as if you swallowed a whole wave at once,
the tightness in your throat
that makes every breath feel borrowed,
and that loud thudding in your ears
your heart reminding you
it's still trying to survive what broke it.

What does it feel like to see him
with someone else?
To watch him laugh the way he once laughed
only with you,
to see him take her to the places
where your stories were written first,
to watch him hold her
with the same tenderness
you once believed was yours alone?

It feels like losing something
you're still holding in your hands.
A quiet pain,

a tear escaping before you even notice,
a sadness buried so deep
it whispers instead of cries.
A hope that lingers
soft, stubborn, impossible
that maybe the universe made a mistake
letting the two of you fall apart.

And then years pass...
you cross paths again
two familiar souls pretending to be strangers.
Does your heart still pull toward him?
Does a piece of you want to run back
to the comfort you once called home?
Or does the ache settle into silence
not anger, not blame
just the understanding
that love changed both of you
in ways words can't explain?

Would you forgive him?
Maybe...
because love always leaves
a gentle place inside you.
Or maybe not
because healing sometimes means
protecting the part of you

that still remembers the hurt.

Some heartbreaks don't disappear.
They soften.
They settle.
They become the sentimental echo
of a love that mattered
a love that shaped you,
even if it didn't stay.

112. When love deepens quietly

You think your heart is full
that you couldn't possibly love
your husband more than you already do.
But then you see him
bending down to their laughter,
holding the little humans
who are half of him
and half of you.

And something shifts.
Something softens.
Something grows.

In the way he wipes tiny tears,
in the way he listens to their stories,
in the way he carries their world
so gently in his hands
you watch him becoming
the kind of father
you always hoped your children would have.

And in those quiet, ordinary moments
your heart melts all over again,

discovering a deeper kind of love
you never knew was waiting.

113. Stay soft, my love

If there's one truth
I want my child to carry,
it's this:

The world won't always play fair.
Not everyone will see
the softness of your heart.
But even then,
you can choose goodness.

Choose grace
when bitterness feels easier.
Choose kindness
when no one is watching,
when no one is clapping.

Choose integrity
in the quiet moments
the ones that reveal
who you truly are.

Because real strength
has never been about winning.
It lives in staying soft,

staying gentle,
staying you,
even when the world
tries its best
to harden you.

114. One last time

That night, I dreamed of him,
as I always do.
Then my phone buzzed.
"Coffee?"

I froze.
My chest tightened.
A message from him...
after all this time...
felt like a cruel, fragile dream.
And then another appeared:
"One last time?"

Months of carrying him inside me
like a quiet ache,
like a secret song no one else could hear...
and now it was real.
Closure.
Finality.
The word alone made me tremble.

I wore my best dress.
Not for me.
Not even entirely for him.

But in some corner of my heart,
I hoped he might remember me
the way I had never stopped
remembering him.

We sat across from each other.
Our favorite coffee between us.
No words.
Nothing needed to be said.
Every glance, every breath,
spoke of the love we once carried
and the pain we could never undo.

Then he held my hand.
Warm. Real. Fleeting.
And whispered goodbye.

And just like that,
everything broke.
I could never dream of him again.
Even in sleep,
even in the dark,
the thought of him
would shatter me,
piece by piece,
leaving nothing but the ache

of someone I will always love,
but can never touch again.

115. Chosen Pain

Loving the one
who breaks me,
bit by bit.

Pouring my whole heart
into hands
that don't know
how to hold it.

And sometimes
even the devil
on my tired shoulder
leans in and whispers,
"What the hell
are you doing
to yourself
now?"

But love...
love makes you stay
long after the pain
has taken a seat
beside you.

Long after the echoes
of your own doubts
grow louder
than your heartbeat.

Yet here I am
choosing the one
who hurts me,
still searching for pieces
of the person
I used to be
before love
became a wound.

116. A quiet ending

No more us,
no more you
no more standing
at the door of a love
that no longer opens.

Our chapter ends
like the last page
of a worn-out book,
softly,
with fingerprints
of everything we once were.

Thank you
for the memories
the laughter,
the warmth,
the little eternities
we borrowed from time.

Some endings
come quietly,
but their afterglow

stays woven
into who we become.

117. It was real for me

It was real for me
every moment, every breath,
every quiet hope I stitched
into the future I imagined with you.

I don't know what it was for you
a passing warmth,
a borrowed feeling,
a chapter you never meant to reread.

But for me...
it was everything.
It meant more than it ever should have,
more than I ever admitted out loud.

I was willing
heart open, hands steady
to choose you in every tomorrow,
to build a forever that felt safe in your name.

And that's what hurts the most:
that my "forever"
was your "for now."
That something so real to me

was only temporary for you.

Yet still,
my heart aches
in the shape of what we could have been.

118. Where we left off

We recognized each other like dawn meets the horizon..
soft, inevitable, a warmth that needed no name.
A memory stirred inside us, ancient and quiet,
as if the universe whispered, you've known this light
before,
and something in our hearts simply opened.

Maybe we come from a life where love paused mid-story,
a chapter left breathing, waiting to be finished.
And now we stand here, finding each other again
two souls returning to a promise time couldn't erase,
ready to continue a love that never truly ended.

119. Unsaid apologies

There were days I held everything together,
and days I wished I could rewrite myself
just to love you better.
If I could open my chest and let you see the truth,
this is what it would whisper:

I'm sorry for the moments
when my patience broke before I did,
when my tiredness became a storm
and you stood in its rain.
I never meant for my exhaustion
to sound louder than my affection.

I'm sorry for every time
my words made you feel small,
or when my silence felt like distance
when all it really was
me fighting battles you never saw.

There were parts of me still hurting,
still learning how to breathe,
still trying to love myself enough
so I could love you the way you deserved.
And somehow, you carried pieces of me

I hadn't even learned to hold.

But please remember this
I never stopped choosing you.
Every late-night fear,
every quiet prayer,
every tiny act I did without saying a word
it was all my heart reaching for you.

No matter how imperfect I was,
or how many times I stumbled,
you remained the place my love returned to,
again and again.

You are, and will always be,
the deepest ache,
the quiet miracle,
the softest part
of my heart.
—Your Mumma

120. The day you return

My heart still hopes for a day yet to come
a quiet moment where the world stands still,
and you step toward me with the softness I remember.

A day when your arms find their way around me,
fitting like a promise finally kept,
and you hold me the way you once did
when home was the space between us.

And in that tender hush,
you whisper the words I've carried for so long
"Thank you for waiting."

121. A lifetime of you

When we're old,
with years folded softly behind us
and memories settling like dust on our skin,
I'll turn to you with a heart still trembling
the way it did the first time we met.

I'll look into your eyes
lined with time, but still the home I chose
and I'll hold your hands as if they're the last truth I
know.
And with a voice full of every lifetime of loving you,
I'll whisper,

"See?
You weren't just a chapter
you were the love
of my entire life."

122. Friends with memories

We met when the world wasn't ready for us,
when time slipped away before our hearts could catch.
Still, I cannot say goodbye
your presence lives in the quiet corners of me,
a ache I carry like a secret I'll never share.

I believe in the "more" that never came,
in the glances that lingered too long,
in the laughter that still echoes through my soul.
Though we remain just friends for now,
a part of me will always love you,
holding onto the what-ifs
that time refused to let us have.

123. Blessed beyond the pain

Maybe life was not as planned,
yet I thank God for every strand
of tears that fell and nights I wept,
for all those storms His grace has kept.

The years of sorrow turn to light,
darkest hours yielding to bright.
Perhaps this joy was meant to stay,
for God knows best, in every way.